Does It Have To Rhyme?

Teaching children to write poetry

Sandy Brownjohn

HODDER AND STOUGHTON

LONDON SYDNEY AUCKLAND TORONTO

British Library Cataloguing in Publication Data

Brownjohn, Sandy
    Does it have to rhyme?
    1. Poetics – Study and teaching – Great Britain
    2. English literature – Study and teaching –
    Great Britain
    I. Title
    808.1   PN1101

ISBN 0 340 25514 5

First published 1980
Ninth impression 1986

Phototypeset in V.I.P. Palatino by
Western Printing Services Ltd, Bristol
Printed and bound in Great Britain for
Hodder and Stoughton Educational,
a division of Hodder and Stoughton Ltd,
Mill Road, Dunton Green, Sevenoaks, Kent,
by J. W. Arrowsmith Ltd, Bristol

CONTENTS

FOR
FITZJOHN'S
PAST AND PRESENT

INTRODUCTION

This book is primarily intended as a handbook for teachers in Junior, Middle and Lower Secondary schools, although some of it may have relevance outside this field. It is my experience that if teachers do not encourage children to write poetry it may be because they do not know where to begin. I have attempted to set out some simple rules and ideas as I have found them applicable to the children I have taught. If they can be of use to other teachers, so much the better.

The chapters in this book are loosely arranged according to the stage a child may have reached. Each one could serve as the basis for at least one class lesson. Chapters 1–6 provide ideas that can be used as ways of encouraging children to want to write. Chapters 7–16 begin to introduce specific techniques and forms as well as ideas which demand more concentrated thought. Chapters 17–25 are more advanced, and as a general rule would only be attempted when the children have had more experience of writing. This is not to say, however, that they need to be followed rigidly. This arrangement serves only as a guide, and many of the ideas can be tried more than once at different stages in the children's development.

A Selected Booklist will be found between pages 94 and 96.

All the examples in this book are written by children aged between nine and eleven years (third and fourth year juniors), and the book is dedicated to them.

I should also like to thank all those who, in one way and another, have given me help and encouragement over the last few years as well as some ideas: particularly Pete Morgan, Kit Wright, Ted Hughes, Alasdair Aston, John Welch, Denis Felsenstein; and special thanks to Evelyn Bourne and, of course, Alan Brownjohn.

1980   *Sandy Brownjohn*

1 POETRY GAMES

I see the teaching of poetry writing to children as the teaching of skills and techniques almost as much as the use of original ideas – a love of language and the excitement of exploring its possibilities, of making it work for you. Children are capable of writing with a high degree of sophistication and control if they are encouraged to do so, and we should beware of those who say it cannot, or should not, be done – they merely wish to keep children 'childish', or save themselves some effort. We must not underestimate what children can do.

To achieve this takes time and enthusiasm. Haphazard or half-hearted lip service to teaching poetry will lay no foundations. It is a constant building on layers of knowledge and practice that brings the rewards.

I make no apology for mentioning the teaching of grammar in connection with some of the poetry games. I feel it is important; and good writing, in the end, should be correct in grammar and spelling. Teaching it this way is not only more enjoyable, but also more relevant. Reading and writing poetry – being steeped in poetry – incidentally introduces and reinforces many aspects of English teaching. I would almost go as far as to say that most necessary skills in English can be taught through poetry at this level.

The following games represent only a few of the ways that can be used to encourage children to think about the meaning of words and to use them adventurously. They are fun to play and can be considered as 'warm-up' exercises before a lesson or as a lesson in itself. It is not a good idea to play more than one (or perhaps two) games in one session. Some of these games can lead directly into poems as will be seen.

The Exquisite Corpse

This game is a version of Consequences and was played by the Dadaists and Surrealists; indeed, it is the surreal quality of the sentences produced which particularly appeals to adults and children alike. There are various ways of playing this game, but the result is always of the same kind.

Each child has a piece of paper on which are drawn several columns. The headings of these can be as follows:

Adjective/Adjective/Noun/Verb/Adjective/Adjective/Noun
or *Adjective/Adjective/Noun/Verb/Adverb/Adjective/Adjective/Noun*

In other words, the column headings stand for the main parts of speech required to make up an interesting sentence. Some work will have to be done to explain the grammatical terms, but the children will soon learn them by playing the game. Because children often have difficulty in understanding each other's handwriting I usually find the following method of play most successful.

Each child writes down five different adjectives in the first column. (It is best to use lined paper as this will help later.) Five seems to be about the right number. The paper is then folded back so that the first column cannot be seen. Now five different adjectives are written in the second column. This is folded back and five nouns are written, and so on until each column has been filled. When completed, the paper is opened out and the resulting sentences are read across the page with definite or indefinite articles inserted where appropriate. Prepositions can also be added and verbs can be put into the required tense and form.

The sentences usually have a bizarre quality which appeals to the children and occasionally produce a phrase or a whole line that is quite remarkable. These can often be used in future poems. It is these fortuitous combinations of words that can help to show children that poetry does not have to be 'long words', but simple words put together in an unusual way.

As will be obvious, the game can also be played a whole line at a time, with each person writing a word in a column, folding it back, and passing the paper on to the next person (more like the game of Consequences).

Adverbs

This is a simple game involving some drama work and can be used to give a clearer understanding of what adverbs are and how they work.

The children sit in a circle while one person leaves the room. Those left behind decide on an adverb on which they all agree (e.g. gloomily). The person outside is called in and must try to guess the adverb. Each child in the circle is asked in turn to illustrate an action in the manner of the adverb. The children might be asked to do simple tasks, like doing up a shoelace, dancing, playing football, writing a letter. While acting them out they must attempt to convey the spirit of the adverb. This forces them to think hard about words and their meanings. Equally, the person guessing has to work at understanding the hints offered.

The Furniture Game

This is another guessing game for a group of children. One person thinks of someone (preferably in the group) but does not say who it is. The rest of the group must guess the name of the person by asking certain sorts of questions. As examples: What piece of furniture is this person? What time of day? What kind of flower? What sort of weather?

The one who has chosen must answer immediately with whatever first comes into his or her head. The answers will give the clues as to who it is. Children are quite remarkable at guessing the names.

This game can be an aid to introducing similes and metaphors since the children are seeing others as totally different things. It can also be carried out as an individual exercise where each child writes about someone in the class using the same criteria.

EXAMPLES

(a) This person is a lampshade.
    She reminds me of a tom cat
    And her colour is a sharp mauve.
    She reminds me of an ashtray
    And if she were a clock she would be at 3 a.m. all
        the time.
    She is a large glass of sherry,
    A mean aunt,
    A double X film,
    And the element fire,
    And she would like the sun to be dedicated to her
        when she dies.

(b) He's a plump Jaffa orange
    And pink pyjamas with white stripes.
    He's a restless labrador jumping onto a sofa.
    He's a wig flying down a laundry chute.
    Placed by the pines and the river he'd be a
        contented moose.
    He's a wooden fence with lots of holes
    And smoke without fire.
    He's a bouncy beachball,
    A brightly coloured clown.

If placed in the sky on a Sunday night he'd become
a U.F.O.
He's an Action Man of Robinson Crusoe.

(c) She's an anxious kingfisher,
She's purple.
If placed in a raging river she becomes an aluminium
canoe.
She stands out to the world as a dining room table.
She's the cold of Alaska and the warmth of Italy,
She's a fox
And a five bar gate.
She's Irish coffee and also vodka.
If she were a boot she'd be trampling down the
rubbish.
She's a country pub in Dorset
And she's the sprinter who works for her crowd.

Lexicon Sentences

This is a game for one to about eight people. A pack of Lexicon
cards (or their equivalent, e.g. Kan-u-go) and a scribe is all that is
needed; or if playing alone a child will have to write down the
results himself. There are many variations of this game and scoring
can be introduced if it is thought necessary. Take out 'Z', and 'Q' is
'wild'.

(a) Each player is dealt five cards and the pack is placed face down
in the centre of the table. (Players may look at their cards.) The
player on the left of the dealer starts by laying any card from his
hand face up on the table. He says a word beginning with that
letter, to begin a sentence. He then replenishes his hand from the
pile in the centre.

The next player plays a card face up on the first card and says a
word, beginning with his letter, which will follow the previous
word and help to build up a sentence. Each player adds to the
sentence in turn. At any point a player can say 'Full stop!' and
begin a new sentence. You are allowed to pass, but the fun is in
using your ingenuity to find a word each time. The game continues
until all the cards are used up.

This game is best played fast: you should not have to think
too long about a word. Obviously there is a chance of some
very interesting phrases and sentences emerging from this
communal effort, but probably its chief value lies in the exercise

of thinking quickly of words and linking them to what has gone before.

(b) Another variation is to lay a certain number of cards face down on the table in a formation, e.g. four rows of eight cards. The second and fourth line might be expected to rhyme. The first card is then turned over and a word said which begins with this letter. The same is done for the next seven cards while the scribe writes down the line as it emerges. This is now the first line of the poem. The same procedure is followed with the next three lines and if rhymes have been decided on, every attempt must be made to achieve them. (A reminder about the sort of words more likely to have a number of possible rhymes may be necessary here. If all else fails you will have to cheat!)

Both of these games involve using words in a novel way which can be fun and yet, at the same time, the children will be increasing their ability to produce words and, we hope, enlarging their vocabulary by learning from other members of the group. A fast reaction can often result in providing words which, though ordinary in themselves, combine to give a phrase of startling originality: the kind of language we are looking for in poetry.

Telegrams

This is a well-known word game which is similar to the lexicon games mentioned above. Most of us probably know S.W.A.L.K. (Sealed With A Loving Kiss) which was put on the backs of envelopes to boyfriends or girlfriends in *much* younger days. There are others, often spelling names of towns or countries, as in the examples used to such effect by Alan Bennett: B.U.R.M.A. and N.O.R.W.I.C.H.

This game consists of printing out the name of a town, county or country, and making up a message, the words of which begin with the letters that spell the name. Teachers can make up their own examples. You might think of it as an exercise in mnemonics!

Questions and Answers

This can be introduced as a game, although I feel it goes beyond that and can lead to some interesting poems. It can be approached in two ways.

(a) Each child writes down five questions of any kind. The

11

children then swap books and each proceeds to answer the questions he has received. The children should be encouraged to be inventive in both questions and answers. The results can be read out round the class and the best can be collected together as a poem. There will probably be a mixture of serious and humorous combinations.

(b) The same results can be obtained if a child writes and answers his own questions. However, there is often marginally more success if the first method is used. Someone else's slant when answering your questions can introduce a more exciting and unexpected element.

EXAMPLES
>What is the sun?
>– The blushing face of the universe.
>Where does the sky begin?
>– Just above the smoke of the factory chimneys.
>Where does Nature part?
>– In the middle years.
>How do you cut the air?
>– With the wind.
>What's inside a hill?
>– Things to come up in the future.
>When is the end of time?
>– When the last cuckoo sinks into Hell.

>How does a window see?
>– Through another window.
>What does a policeman do when he's alone?
>– Learns to be a man.
>How does the moon cry?
>– With a hanky in his hand.
>Why do dogs have four legs?
>– They had to put their hair somewhere.
>Is life a dream?
>– Mine is.

Written by children aged 10 years

Preferences

This game is played with two teams. One team is the 'Hates' and the other is the 'Likes' (or 'Loves'). A subject is chosen to which people may have strong reactions, either positive or negative, and the teams line up opposite one another. They then take it in turns to shout to each other about the subject in the following way.

Let us take the subject of holidays – not perhaps, on the surface, something that children might dislike, but worth a try. The first member of the 'Loves' might shout – 'What I love about holidays is that I can go swimming every day.' The first member of the 'Hates' might reply – 'What I hate about holidays is it always rains.' The second member of the 'Loves' – 'What I love about holidays is being able to stay in bed.' The second member of the 'Hates' – 'What I hate about holidays is having to stay with Auntie Jean.'

This continues with every member of each team contributing a line when it is his or her turn. Other subjects that might be interesting are, Spiders, Jelly, Winter, Neighbours and Mirrors, and of course anything else you care to try. It may be necessary for the groups to discuss the subject first of all to allow each team member to write down his or her line. This ensures that everyone has a different thing to say and also makes the final effort run freely without awkward pauses.

It is quite good to write all the lines down to make a poem. The particular benefit gained from this exercise is the practice it gives in thinking about a subject in as many different ways as possible (see also Chapters 10 and 17, pages 35 and 49). This will provide the children with a useful approach to writing their poems later. It can help to give depth and more interesting angles so that they do not all write the same thing – rather boring if you have to mark them! (See Edwin Morgan's poem 'A View of Things' which can be found in *Junior Voices, the third book.*)

Prepositions

This is another game which provides the added bonus of teaching some grammar in a painless way. It is best to have some discussion as to what prepositions are and to write on the blackboard all the prepositions the children suggest, e.g. before, behind, beside, round, under, over. The game can then be played in two ways.

(a) Making a communal poem
A subject is selected, e.g. 'my head' or 'the window', and each child writes one line beginning with a preposition. The sort of lines written might be as follows: 'Inside my head are caves I can't explore', or 'Below the soft sand is the dead water'. The children then read the lines one after the other producing an instant poem.

One of the great benefits of this game is that the children are made aware of all the different angles you can take on a particular subject. It should help them to look at something in greater depth and, of course, it highlights a particular part of speech and should both heighten their awareness and extend their use of prepositions.

(b) Making individual poems
The second way of using prepositions is to ask each child to write a poem either using the same formula as above, or using the prepositions as a stepping-off point for the poem.

EXAMPLES

The Window

Outside the window there are impressions,
These are impressions of the outside world.
Inside looks outside and outside looks in.
My range of sight has grown because of this.

Next to the window there are some curtains,
These curtains are ready to block my view.
From outside it seems to be a mirror
When these curtains are drawn from the inside.

Inside the window there is one big piece
Made of all the colours of the spectrum.
The dark blue of night, the turquoise of day,
The green of the grass and the red of blood.

Throughout the window there is life and death
Showing the life of the outside beings.
Outside the people just look in at us,
It is more than just glass. The curtains close.

Alex Gollner

Looking at the World

Behind my back the world spins like a top,
My back faces towards a life and death.
You in front of me, are behind me too.
The world's behind me, I am behind myself.

Beneath my feet the ants are making a maze,
Down by the earth's core lava forms and erupts,
It melts, cools, and is the rock it once was.
Like gushing water my feet run madly.

Over my head man builds a concrete jungle
For us to be born, to live and die in.
Far away the sun shines hot and brightly,
But here I sit staring, staring at you.

Michael Corti

Behind my Head

Behind my head time passed by in haste,
Throughout the turning of my head it ended.
Without time I grew old hair and wrinkles.
Through my life time started and finished.
Behind my head the wood rotted far away,
Across one leg lay a decaying white rose,
Outside, the woodworms chewed at my case.

Richard Ball

Prepositions

Behind my head lives sadness without life,
Between my head swims a paradise world,
Around my head lie clouds dizzy from the wind.
Far from my head are shadows melting quickly,
Beside my head stands another head
Reflecting.

Catriona Ferguson

2 ALLITERATION

I usually introduce the technique of alliteration in the very first lesson with a class. The alliterative content is done to excess in this exercise but this is in order to 'capture' the children's interest and let them feel that poetry is enjoyable. It can be explained that alliteration is most effective if used sparingly when they come to write poems in the future.

The children are asked to write a sentence for each number up to ten, or further if they wish. Most of the words in a sentence will begin with the same sound which takes its lead from the initial sound of the number, e.g. 'One wakeful walrus wondered if whiting could waltz, Two tremulous tomatoes tried to tickle a tench.'

The children should be encouraged to use a dictionary – you will need one for every child, and ideally, different formats and levels to give wider choice. The beauty of the sentences is their nonsense and their almost surreal element, and this means that children can be encouraged to use new words found in the dictionary without having to worry too much whether they have used them correctly. This will help to make them more adventurous in the future and give them a love of the sounds of words. If they use a word in the wrong part of speech it is very easy to show them gently the correct form (commenting meanwhile on the choice of such a good word!). It is also clear that this exercise can be used to help children grow more familiar with, and find their way around in, a dictionary – making it more like a game than a daunting task.

Give some examples beforehand, but not too many; there is good reason for going once through the exercise on the board with the whole class before asking the children to work individually. You will then have the opportunity to say that although 'Six silly sausages sat on smelly socks' is funny, it would probably be improved by some more unusual words!

EXAMPLE

One waggly walrus won a wet wager,
Two trustful twins tumbled into a typhoon,
Three thin thoroughbreds thumped a thick thief,
Four fiddly ferns ferociously ate a ferret,
Five fervent fleas sat famished in a farm,
Six shy shuttlecocks swam in shampoo,
Seven stupid strawberries sinned on a stripey
    stretcher,
Eight echoing earthquakes exterminated an eclipse,
Nine nosy nomads knitted knotted knickers,
Ten topless toffees told a tale.

Written by children aged 9 years

3 I SHOULD LIKE TO . . .

The idea for this came from the poem 'To Paint the Portrait of a Bird' by Jacques Prévert (translated by Lawrence Ferlinghetti) which can be found in the anthology Touchstones 3. Briefly, this poem says that you paint a cage with an open door and place the canvas against a tree. Then you must hide and wait for a bird to enter the cage. As soon as it does you paint the door closed and paint out all the bars. Then you must paint certain things to make the bird sing:

> . . . the green foliage and the wind's freshness
> the dust of the sun
> and the noise of the insects in the summer heat.

It was this part of the poem that gave me the idea of asking the children to write about things they would like to do, which could not normally be done – for example, to hear things you could only normally see, touch or taste, and to see sounds, to taste smells, or touch tastes, although it was not confined solely to the senses. They were asked to write for each 'wish' and to expand the description of it to make each picture more vivid.

I find this particularly useful as an exercise in the first few lessons with a class since it acts as a key to open up their fantasy. When I read them the Prévert poem at least two-thirds of the class always says it isn't possible. But once they are off their very rational plane and into this more fantastic world they soon begin to enjoy the idea. It opens up marvellous possibilities and paves the way for more interesting writing in the future. With all the barriers down and the constraints of the real world forgotten, the children are free to experiment with words and ideas.

EXAMPLES

I would like to paint the noise of a vulture on the eastern
    mountains on a summer's evening,
The buzz of the dragonflies on the marsh,
The sound of a humming bird's wings as they go up and
    down in a plant.

I should like to take home the rays of the moon on a
    frosty night,
The crinkle of the willows on the lake at the bottom of
    the world.
I should like to touch the magic of the witch in Hell.
I should like to hear dew on the grass on a cold winter's
    morning,
The painter's brush wipe on the canvas,
The glow in a tiger's eye on a very dark night,
The calling of a painting to an artist.
I should like to understand the ways of the gods of
    ancient Mexico,
The animals' thoughts of being locked up in a zoo in the
    Saturday noise,
The mystery of the dark,
And the paint in the tin, waiting to be mixed.

Roddy Mattinson

I should like to paint the snowflakes' hearts which are
    beating away to the second,
The disobedience of a flag that won't flutter in the
    breeze,
The heat of a candle in the middle of the night,
The happiness of a merry-go-round which has started
    spinning,
The coldness in an iceberg's fast running blood,
The hyena's hysterical laugh when it howls at night.

Daniel Phillips

I should like to paint the mating call of the bluetit,
The swan's death cry after a duel with a brother.
I should like to feel the happiness of a thrush when he is
    warmed by the sun,
The sound of a clumsy cockroach awakening in the
    morning dew,
I should like to take home the sound of the rushing weir.
I would like to see the whistling of the wind,
I would like to listen to the growing of the corn.

Louis Lyne

I should like to touch the song of the skylark wavering
    on the horizon
Or feel the stars in the night sky.
I would love to keep the moon shimmering in a jar.
I would like to hear the sound of the past
Or paint the liberty of life.
I would like to hear the frenzy of a mad lizard
And keep the future in a box.
I should like to see the scream of a monkey rebounding
    in the jungle.
I would like to hear the sunset going down below the
    hills
And see the donkey braying in the fields,
Also to hear the elderberry tree flowering in the Spring.
I would like to paint the second in which the honeybee
    dies.

Rebecca Luff

4 COLLECTIVE NOUNS

Discussing collective nouns also belongs, I feel, to the first few lessons with a class. It is another way of playing with words which can be enjoyable, and also less demanding on slow workers whom you do not want to 'lose' because they find the sheer grind of writing too much. Later, when you have their interest completely, they will probably miraculously find they can write much faster and so much more!

All the children do is make up their own collective nouns. Preparation for this naturally involves explaining what nouns are, and the different categories. It would be well to test the children's own knowledge of existing collective nouns and add to these others they may not know.

But then I always point out that these are so well known and overused that they are no longer fresh. It is now that you ask the children to make up new ones of their own – collections of anything. This involves their exploring the nature of the things they choose and thinking about the meaning of words very carefully if they are to find successful combinations. The best of these can then be illustrated in pictures, music, or drama.

EXAMPLES

a coil of pythons	an eruption of wildebeeste
a bask of cats	a lag of tortoises
a gossamer of spiders	a wheel of smoke
a haystack of light	an echo of whispers
a diminution of ants	a Speaker's Corner of mouths

Following on from this, it can be good to make a list of all the best new collective nouns and ask the children to choose one as the title for a poem which they then write. By giving them a choice you will probably find that there is something in the list that will appeal to each child and there is also something special about the choices having been written by them originally. It encourages them to feel that their ideas are worthwhile, which will help to give them confidence in their writing.

EXAMPLES

A Lock of Secrets

I hesitate to unlock secrets,
A long echo of whispers does it for me.
A dream of silence flares on my body
For I have disobeyed my secret.
A mask of darkness covers my view –
I strike it with light.

Charles De'Ath

A Team of Crickets

The crickets are
Icy, unpleasant,
Jumpy and small,
Green with anger and envy
Of the pretty caterpillar,
On the oak leaf,
That turns into the
Magnificent butterfly

Michele Collins

A Cloud of Gravel

Up in the air a cloud of gravel cried,
'My dream's come true – I can fly!'
It flew for miles and miles,
Landed on unfriendly grass
And was chased off

Jason Sewards

A Dream of Silences

Silence,
Where is it?
Always being broken,
Never kept.
Silence is a dream
For us to look for,
To seek,
To keep.

Jane Alden

A Planet of Dust

A planet of dust
Not wanted among the kings of air.
Made to be blown away by the human breath,
Trapped by the skin of a local cat.

Tony Reed

5 SYNONYMS AND NAMES

Since one of the things we are obviously trying to do is build up a child's vocabulary and widen the experience and use of words, I have always found it useful to do some work on synonyms. One of the points I am constantly making to children is that, if possible, it is best to avoid using a particular word more than once, unless it is absolutely unavoidable or repetition is intended. To have to find other ways of saying the same thing is a good exercise and it trains the mind for later work. I have also found that it helps towards giving the children an enthusiasm for, and love of, words.

There is now a good thesaurus available for Junior and Middle schools called *The Word Hunter's Companion* by James Green (see booklist, page 96), and I would recommend that there should be at least half a dozen in the classroom, and a class set if possible. However, in addition to that, it can be very useful if each child makes his or her own Thesaurus. A class session, once or twice a week, is a good idea, when the children suggest a word for which as many synonyms, or near synonyms, are found as possible. The words are written in a list with the headword at the top. An index can be kept at the front and all the pages numbered. A good word with which to begin these books is 'to speak' as there are literally tens of words that could be included.

Another way of displaying this word-hunting is to draw diagrams with the main word written large in the centre. It can be useful to draw a series of circles or hexagons, like a honeycomb, and write the words into the spaces. They can be called charts, and different colours can be allotted to each part of speech: red for nouns, blue for adjectives, say.

This can also be done for antonyms where a line is drawn down the centre of the chart. The synonyms are written one side of the line and the antonyms on the other side.

A related exercise is that of making up names for people. I find it very tedious to read the names of brothers, sisters and classmates in the children's writing, in what are essentially explorations into fantasy. Although I can see that these familiar names probably give the children a secure base and, as it were, a lifeline back to reality, by the time they have reached nine or ten years of age they should be capable of entering these fantasy worlds with more unusual

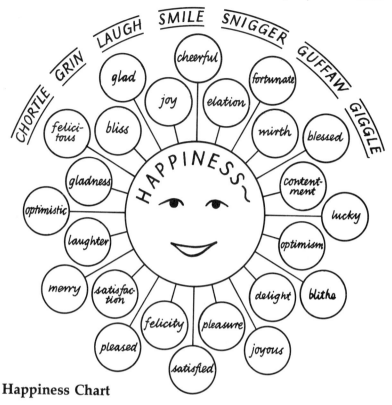

Happiness Chart

people! I ask the children to make up a list of names for different sorts of people.

EXAMPLES

Colonel 'Shorty' Anstruther

The Rev. Thomas Langland

Lady Deborah Trinket-Smythe

Penny Popplethwaite

Cynthia Masters

Steve Parker

Sid Fortesque

Boris Bircham

If nothing else, this is fun to do and also to follow up by giving a short character sketch of each one. What's in a name? Well, we are all likely to have an instant mental picture of someone about whom we know nothing except the name. Names do carry some weight and there is no doubt that people often seem to have names that suit them; or perhaps they grow into their names? However, this can be thought of as a game, although it may help children's writing generally.

6 NEW WORDS FOR OLD

This is something to be done during the first few weeks of taking a class and is more for enjoyment than anything else. The main advantage is that it can help the children towards gaining a love of words, and of playing with words, which is essential if they are going to write well.

In the past shepherds who were out with their flocks all day would evolve new personal counting systems for counting their sheep. It was probably one way of passing the time. Some of these kinds of systems can be found on the first twenty pages of the four books of *Junior Voices* in the bottom right-hand and left-hand corners – for example, een 1, teen 2, tuther 3, futher 4, and fip 5. Children can enjoy making up their own counting systems.

Also in *Junior Voices, the third book* there are some poems by Alastair Reid with the titles 'Squishy Words (to be said when wet)', 'Bug Words (to be said when grumpy)', and 'Sounds', which invent words for the sounds that things actually make. In *Junior Voices, the second book* we find 'Mean Song' by Eve Merriam which also makes up words, and of course we have 'Jabberwocky' by Lewis Carroll from *Through the Looking-Glass*.

All these can be read to the children for pleasure, but may also lead them to want to make up their own words. They could write words to be said when happy, when singing in the bath, when stroking the cat, when you've just fallen in the mud, and so on. They might also write a longer poem on the lines of 'Jabberwocky' and go on to give an explanation of what their made-up words mean, as Humpty Dumpty does in Chapter Six of *Through the Looking-Glass*.

7 A B C BOOKS

This idea derives from those ABC books we were all probably given when young, which have a page for every letter of the alphabet. There might be: 'A is for Apple so rosy and red', or 'C is for cat with a long fluffy tail'. Each page would contain an illustration of the object and was aimed at teaching us to recognise letters and words.

However, making ABC books with older children can take on a very different aspect. When we did it the children were nine and ten years old. I explained what we were going to do, but that our words and illustrations were going to be much more adult in their approach. We started with every child writing a sentence for any letters of the alphabet they wanted to use; the only condition was that one important word – a noun, adjective, verb or adverb – had to begin with the letter they had chosen. We then sorted through all the sentences and grouped them under themes. The themes that emerged were War, Life and Death, Mystery and Religion, Fears and Feelings, and Animals.

We chose one sentence for each letter under these headings, wrote them on a large sheet of paper and noted the gaps. The children wrote more sentences to fill these gaps. When the lists were complete each child chose which sentences he or she wanted to illustrate and these pictures were done in an abstract style. They tried to feel the essence of the meaning and to translate this into shape, colour and texture in their paintings. When everything was finished we made the pictures and sentences up into books.

The whole project took some time to complete and was greatly enjoyed. The paintings improved as time went on and the children broke much new ground as well as totally integrating their painting with their writing.

EXAMPLES

A for an apple left to rot away.
B for the bitterness in every person's life.
N is a nephew murdered in a moonlit house.
P for the padlock that locks spirit in.
Q for the long queues waiting to die.
A is the army ambling through the lone fields.
E is extermination.
*I*nk is the blood of the pen.
Q quivers quietly in the corner.
T is the tangled barbed wire blocking fences.

8 COLOURS

Children are always being asked to write about colours from the time they first enter the infant school. The writing usually takes the form of 'What is Blue?' or 'What is Red?' and the poems that result have a rather uniform quality. That is fine for the younger children, but can become very tedious by the time children are eight years and over. We have probably all read the kind of poem that goes like this:

> Blue is the colour of the sea,
> Blue is the summer sky,
> Blue is my budgerigar,
> Blue is a bluebell,
> Blue is the little butterfly . . .

I decided to write about colours with a class of ten year olds but I wanted the results to be different. We began with a short discussion of how colours are used in some sayings. For example, *Red* for anger, embarrassment, danger; *Green* for envy, go, inexperience; *Yellow* for cowardice; *White* for fright. It was decided that the only mention of the colour would be in the title – the purpose being to prevent the repetition of, 'Blue is, blue is . . .' The children were asked to write about things which this colour made them think of, and not necessarily things which *were* the colour. It was, therefore, a more abstract approach, attempting to get at the essence of colour, its effect and the feelings it aroused. After talking about this to the children I found they readily set to work and entered into the spirit of it. After they had written the poems they did some abstract paintings based on the same idea.

The whole project was a success: it involved all the children in some deep thinking about words, shapes, thoughts and feelings, and made them aware of the other dimensions possible when dealing with a subject.

EXAMPLES

Black

The old mine degenerating in the dead of night,
The exposed body lying helplessly on the ground,
An engulfing darkness in a maze of winding
    passages,
The dagger of evil stained with blood,
A cold and lingering silence.

Else Thompson

Black

The misleading dark mist grazing the moor,
The day drowned by the night's darkness,
The scattered dolorous graves in the graveyard,
An evil mind furiously thinking,
A terrorising thunder beating down rain,
The silent and still spirit.

Clare Dowell

Green

The icy day gloomy and still,
The deep full mind,
A handful of leaves in a forgotten place,
A seagull hopelessly flies into mist,
An eagle flying from a cloud, lost in a full deep
    shallow.

Jamie McGowan

Green

The sun shining through the leaves on the trees,
The eerie mist rising from the mountains,
A storm approaching from the south coast,
An endless night looming through a window,
An arrow leaping from the darkness.

Steve Webber

Turquoise

The mystic beauty of freedom,
The majestic silence of a deserted house,
The awesome splendour of a long built palace,
A precious gem glinting in a shaded corner,
The magical glow of love,
The howling of a lonely wolf.

Mischa Twitchin

Red

The forgotten hero lies on the battlefield,
The miners are trapped in subterranean passages
Crying for help,
A fire is lit and the flames are burning wood.

Nicholas Lee

Yellow

The opening way to happiness,
Warmth pertaining to wideness,
A revolving shadow,
An empty view,
A philanthropist,
The tardy wind carrying the leaves.

Diagoro Isobe

9 ACROSTICS

An acrostic is a poem in which the first (or last) letters of each line spell a word or sentence.

EXAMPLE

Lobster

L ate in the evening my claws are sharp and ready,
O n the sea in my shell I wait.
B efore my claws will open I will polish them till they shine.
S agging in the mist, a starfish is asleep
T hough I will wait till my enemy comes.
E vening stars brighten the green waters, but still I wait.
R etaining my courage, I see the crab slowly scampering
over.

Steven Gregory

This introduces a limitation, small though it is, which requires the children to think just that much harder about the words they use. It often results in more interesting words and inversions which can contribute to the success of a poem. In the example above, how much more impact is made by such lines as:

'On the sea in my shell I wait',

or:

'Sagging in the mist, a starfish is asleep'.

Were Steven to have written 'I wait in my shell on the sea', the line would not have been so effective, although this might well have been what he would have written had there been no need to begin with the letter 'O'. Similarly, the word 'sagging' may never have suggested itself, but there is no doubt that it is successful, particularly as it is placed in a prominent position at the beginning of the line.

This is a popular exercise with the children and extremely valid, I feel. It presents an obstacle which it is possible to surmount, yet at the same time it effectively slows their writing up and demands extra thought. This can only be good because too often children write down the first thing that enters their heads and are then content to leave it. There are times, of course, when the spontaneous and immediate thoughts are most successful and .nis should not be forgotten; but, as a general rule, I have found that the deeper they can think about an idea the better the results.

Some children will naturally learn to go back to a poem and 're-work' it, putting in revisions and improvements, but with most children we need actively to encourage this approach. One way of doing this is to provide other different frameworks and technical limitations with which they can experiment. Many of these are dealt with in later chapters.

EXAMPLES

Catalogue

C atalogue –
A s you know,
T his has
A rticles listed in it.
L ooking for something?
O h, then look in this book.
G ood for you, there is everything here.
U ncertain? Trust us.
E verything O.K.?

Diagoro Isobe

Atoms

A lways within a finger's touch,
T errible murderers swallow us up,
O bnoxious beings prepare us for war and
M ushrooms grow where we are dropped.
S ee us tessellate under a slide.

Louis Lyne

Enormous

E nlarged to great extent,
N o end to bigger than big,
O r no start to smaller than small.
R adiantly, a huge heaven surrounding
M eant growing in fame and shrinking in age.
O utnumbered by no-one, nothing but itself,
U nited to all being creatures.
S oulless but living in voice.

Andrew Hall

Catkin

C rave of beauty and elegance
A bundantly growing to bring life,
T hat brings not evil but sweet smells,
K iss of life to earth.
I ts softness idly bending in the breeze,
N atural colours that gleam in the sunlight.

Stephen Bailey

(See also 'Caterpillar', page 75; and 'Moustache', page 52.)

10 RIDDLES

There are many examples of riddles to be found in the anthologies available to schools (notably in the books of *Junior Voices* and *Voices*). Many of them are translations from Anglo-Saxon. Most children enjoy riddles; they love guessing games.

Riddles generally seem to fall into two categories. There are the sort that spell the answer, a letter a line. For example:

> My first is in *b*ook but not in cover,
> My second in *s*ister but not in brother,
> My third is in *r*ain but not in sun,
> My fourth is in brea*d* but not in bun.

There are quite often one or two lines at the end of these which give a clue to the whole word.

The second sort are veiled and interesting descriptions of the subject which provide enough information and clues without giving the answer away too easily. Rhyme is often used, but near rhymes can be just as effective (e.g. 'cover' and 'brother'). The lines of a riddle also have a 'magical' quality about them: something of the element of chants and spells and of the impossible being possible. It is present in the old song 'I will give my love an apple', and can also be seen in the following riddle.

> In marble halls as white as milk,
> Lined with a skin as soft as silk,
> Within a fountain crystal-clear,
> A golden apple doth appear.
> No doors there are to this stronghold,
> Yet thieves break in and steal the gold.

> *Traditional English*
> (ଃଃ૩)

One of the benefits of asking children to write riddles is that, since they are not allowed to mention the subject, they are forced to think harder about it. They must choose their words carefully so as not to make it too easy to guess, and they must search out the hidden aspects of the subject, thus looking at it probably more closely than they ever have before. Being able to find other ways of expressing what might be a commonplace object will be of great value later on in other poems. In the example above the 'yolk' of the egg is called 'a golden apple' and the 'shell' is the 'stronghold'. These are imaginative descriptions of the kind that we hope will give the children practice for their future writing. And there are the beautiful contradictions which often add to the power of riddles, and other poems too. For example:

> No doors there are to this stronghold,
> Yet thieves break in and steal the gold.

and

> I will give my love a palace wherein she may be
> And she may unlock it without e'er a key.

EXAMPLES

> Often talked of, never seen,
> Ever coming, never been,
> Daily looked for, never here,
> Still approaching ever near.
> Thousands for my presence wait,
> But by the decree of fate,
> Though expected to appear,
> They will never see me here.

Andrew Hall
(The Future)

> I am a stone but not a stone,
> I occur in flocks and am never alone.
> A nebula of falling lights
> Which dive at earth like tiny kites.
> I sometimes pain but rarely kill,
> I pound and thump like a minute drill.
> Occasionally floods I cause,
> I plummet down with tremendous force.
> The traces of my presence are seldom clear,
> I merely change my shape and disappear.

Adam Lyne
(Hailstones)

I'm isolated to the rest of the world.
Some say I'm mean,
Some say it's natural,
Although I'm never seen.
I steal day and night,
I'm usually unknown,
Sometimes I'm fast, sometimes slow,
And I always come alone.
I'm all over the world
And in space,
I'm mass and single.
I happen in one place.

Steve Webber
(Death)

My metal coat is hard,
My body substance a white smooth cream,
My head you must screw on tight.
Morn and noon and night,
Each day I'm losing weight.
They rob me for their bristles
To fulfill my pasted fate.

Jason Turner
(Toothpaste)

11 HAIKU

Haiku is a Japanese form which consists of three lines of seventeen syllables. The first line has 5 syllables, the second 7 and the third 5. These Haiku are small poems which somehow manage to say much more than would seem possible in so few words.

They are quite easy for children to write and are best described as small 'snapshots' which capture a moment and feeling and, if possible, can comment in a wider sense about life or the spirit of the subject. Because they are so short, all children can attempt them and feel successful (which is very important). The poems have an almost childlike simplicity, although to write a very good one is harder than it may appear. They can be illustrated and make a good display on the wall or in a book. Using school instruments, some children may also wish to compose short pieces of music to illustrate their poems. These pieces can be played as an accompaniment to a reading of the Haiku (a useful idea for assemblies for those teachers who are obliged to arrange such things!).

To explain a syllable, equate it with a 'beat' in music and sound out some of the children's names – it is easiest to use the fingers of one hand to tap out the 'beats'. Although children will wish to have the correct number of syllables in each line – 5, 7, 5 – I do not feel this to be absolutely necessary. The main object is to write short lines where every word counts. Children should be told to write about one thing only at a time, to concentrate their thoughts on their chosen idea and to describe it in such a way as to make it interesting and vivid to the reader.

EXAMPLES

The goat eats this,	(4)
The goat eats that,	(4)
Brandishing his beard.	(5)

Michael Corti

A kingdom of birds,	(5)
The voice of wings fluttering,	(7)
A tune gathering.	(5)

Andrew Hall

The cup fills.	(3)
It lies on its side	(5)
And bathes in lukewarm water.	(6)

Adam Lyne

Tramp

Sam is lying here	(5)
A silhouette of yellow dust.	(8)
This will be his home.	(5)

Louis Lyne

There are many examples of translations from the Japanese to be found in the *Voices* and *Touchstones* anthologies, and in *The Penguin Book of Japanese Verse* edited by Anthony Thwaite and Geoffrey Bownas.

One of the great lessons to be drawn from writing Haiku is that choosing words carefully, to express as much as possible, should be carried over into all writing. Here also is an opportunity to point out the importance of titles. I believe that, where possible, a title should add something to a poem and, with Haiku, the extra syllables you can gain by giving a title can be very useful.

12 TANKA

Tanka is another Japanese form of poem and is almost like an extension of the Haiku. It has 5 lines of 31 syllables used in the following way: 5, 7, 5, 7 and 7. Like Haiku and Cinquains (see Chapter 13) it limits the writer within the strict confines of the form and can serve the same useful purpose of making the children choose their words carefully to express 'much-in-little' as the Muskrat would say in *The Mouse and his Child*!

With Tanka it is probably more necessary to adhere to the form than it is with Haiku where I feel the children can be a little freer. An explanation of how to count syllables and perhaps one or two class efforts, or your own, would be enough to give them the idea, especially if they have already written some Haiku, which I think would be advisable.

EXAMPLES

Tree

Swaying in the wind
I catch people's attention.
I begin to wave,
They never wave back to me.
I think nobody likes me.

Dominic Dowell

Singing

I'm singing my song,
The words slipping through my lips
Meet their waiting ears,
Then fall into memory
To be whistled out again.

Matthew Festenstein

Across I travel,
Desolate and cold it is.
My shadow follows.
Just whistling to pass the time –
It helps when you're so lonely.

Christian Tattersfield

13 CINQUAINS

A *Cinquain* is a short poem whose form was invented by an American poet with the memorable name of Adelaide Crapsey. It is a kind of English Haiku or Tanka and somehow fits our English rhythms better. The form of a Cinquain is 5 lines of 22 syllables: 2, 4, 6, 8 and 2. If the children are already familiar with counting syllables it will be very easy to introduce this new form to them, otherwise see Chapter 11 on Haiku. The short last line with only two syllables needs to make some impact. As with Haiku and Tanka the limitations of the form force the children to use words carefully and to convey the meaning clearly. The lines can run on and it is often better if they do. The rhythm should be predominantly iambic (as in 'What *is* this *life* if *full* of *care*'), but this is not essential, and may only confuse the children if you insist on it.

EXAMPLES

Mr Death at the Door

Butler,
Open up for
It is Mr Death come
To see how well I am doing.
How kind!

Rebecca Bazeley

The Dreamer

Dreamer,
What do you see
In that pot of dreams you
Hold? I see nothing you can't see
But you.

Rebecca Bazeley

Barbershop Quartet

I saw
Four alley cats
Sitting in tin dustbins
And banging the lids together
Loudly.

Callum Crawford

The Trees

I saw
Two old oak trees
Playing with a ball. One
Threw it in the other's branches
And laughed.

Jane Alden

News Flash

News Flash:
An elephant
Was seen walking over
The queen at Buckingham Palace.
She died.

Anthony Wakefield

14 GRAVESTONES

Although the theme may seem morbid, it is a fact that children often write about death. This exercise manages to capture their imaginations as well as to encourage them to learn something from history which they may not have interested themselves in before.

The idea originates from the *Spoon River Anthology* by Edgar Lee Masters which contains poems written from the viewpoint of deceased inhabitants of Spoon River. Some of these are reproduced in *Story, the third book*, or can be read in the original.

Children *can* make up names and dates of imaginary persons, but another idea is to visit an old churchyard and collect real names. (An interesting diversion here is to look out for epitaphs which are often found on older gravestones or on tablets inside a church.) The children then write poems about the life and death of these people, as if the people themselves were speaking. Details of the period can be included to make the poems more authentic; particularly a study of the social conditions will help to add colour. Some class discussion may be useful for this, especially if it 'ties in' with a particular history project being studied at the time. It may indeed lead into a class project.

In many smaller villages whole generations of families are buried in the churchyard and the same surnames recur. This may lead to a sequence of poems about one family. It can be very effective if the poems are written out on paper cut to the shape of a gravestone and even coloured to look like stone – mosses, lichen and all.

It is probably unnecessary to advise caution, but teachers should be aware of any recent deaths in a child's family. It may not be appropriate for some children, although I know of at least one child who found a great release in writing about a grandfather who had recently died. It is also possible that a visit to a previously unknown graveyard would be better than to one which is local and may be full of associations for some children.

EXAMPLES

STAN HARTLEY
1701–1761

My son I brought from London,
Bill was his name,
But soon I joined him in his grave.
A retreating death I had,
A war against the Scottish rebellion.
I died, forced back at Heptonstall.
They came up from behind.

Daniel Rubin

BILL HARTLEY
1747–1758

A Cockney man I was.
Bill Hartley my name.
At 4 I came to live at Heptonstall,
But not for long.
I soon became sieved
Because I was struck with Hepton Church by lightning,
And buried where I died.

Daniel Rubin

STELLA HARTLEY
1779–1804

Where were my savers
When danger was near?
They never helped anyone.

I don't need friends where I lie
Beneath the rock where I fell.

That strange wind force
I suffer from now
By myself in my earth bound cell.

Petra Coveney

15 EPITAPHS

There are many examples of epitaphs in a number of poetry anthologies (notably *The Faber Book of Epigrams and Epitaphs* edited by Geoffrey Grigson), and many of them are amusing. They either comment on the person's life, the character, the profession or the manner of death, and often incorporate a play on words.

EXAMPLES

> Here lies one who for medicine would not give
> A little gold, and so his life he lost:
> I fancy now he'd wish again to live
> Could he but guess how much his funeral cost
>
> *Anon.*

Fleet Street Epitaph

> Go tell our master, all you passers by,
> That here, obedient to his laws, we lie.

On King Charles the Second

> Here lies our Sovereign Lord the King,
> Whose word no man relies on;
> Who never said a foolish thing,
> Nor ever did a wise one.
>
> *John Wilmot, Earl of Rochester*

A good exercise is for the children to write epitaphs for a type of person or a well-known character (fictional characters can be included). As many examples as possible should be read to the class before they begin, to illustrate the nature of epitaphs. Discussion of the various ways they might use to begin their poems might also be helpful. For example, 'Here lies . . .', 'Beneath this ground/stone/earth . . .', 'Beneath your feet . . .'

One of the problems that arises here is that of rhyme, as most epitaphs do rhyme. If you have not encouraged rhyme, it may be necessary to discuss its use with the children in order to prevent the really silly things that they can present you with. It may be that you will wish to delay this idea until rhymes, internal rhymes, and near rhymes have been dealt with and the children have more experience in using them. (See Chapter 24, page 72.)

EXAMPLES

Grave Words

Here he lies in sleep –
He does not snore.

Alex Gollner

To a Chess Champion

Here lies a chess player,
He's played his last game,
For he who you walk upon
Has been checkmated again.

Matthew Festenstein

To a Dustman

Here he lies this poor chap,
Been cleaning since a kid.
He was really quite all right
Until he flipped his lid.

Matthew Festenstein

16 REINCARNATION

This is always a fascinating subject, whether you believe it is possible or not. Its introduction here is merely as an imaginative exercise. The word exists and its meaning can be explained and the concept presented as a hypothesis which need not be taken too seriously if you do not wish it.

Some class discussion about reincarnation as a possible reality can be interesting and enlightening, but the final object is to write a poem. Each child can look at the task from a variety of angles. Either *he* is to be born again, or a relative, friend, famous person, fictional character, or an imaginary person. The idea is to describe what the person would return as, possibly *choose* to be reborn as, were the opportunity to arise. Anything should be eligible, both animate and inanimate, real and abstract. The poems can be serious or humorous. The most surprising poems can result from a lively discussion, as the first example below shows. It seemed to appear from nowhere after a session when one child asserted that her mother would come back as a telephone because she talked non-stop, and a whole group of children were convinced that a girl's uncle was a chicken they could see in a field.

EXAMPLES

Re-incarnation

When he came back he came in a carriage of numbers.
The carriage was made of every number.
Every number except the number 4,
It was inside.
Yet this 4 was different.
Different from every other 4,
Every other number.
It is alive. In every possible way it is 4th.
It is 4th at cleverness, 4th at stupidity.
It is 4th at riding, 4th at walking.
Everything it touches assumes the form of a 4.
Nobody knows him, but everyone now looks similar.

Donal Crawford

Reborn

The song of my heart no longer is within me,
My hands no longer hold my life,
My story is to be told but that is behind me,
But this part of me starts with an empty page
Which is yet to be written.
Somebody spare me, whoever is there.

Miles Greene

17 'THIRTEEN WAYS OF LOOKING AT A BLACKBIRD'

To those who already know Wallace Stevens' 'Thirteen Ways of Looking at a Blackbird' (from his *Collected Poems*, published by Faber and Faber) it will be obvious where the idea for this exercise originated. How many ways are there of looking at something? I suppose the answer to that question is there are as many as you can find.

The object, then, is that the children choose a subject and try to look at it from many different angles. I suggest six or more is the best to start with, although it is as well to discourage the too ambitious from attempting ninety-nine ways! On the other hand, that could be interesting.

Obviously this should stretch their imaginations and make them work for their poems. As with many of the other ideas in this book, this should encourage, indeed force, the children to examine their chosen subjects in far greater depth, which will be good practice for all their writing. The resulting flexibility of mind, and the ability to see things from different angles, cannot but help their approach to other things besides poetry.

EXAMPLE

Six Ways of Looking at the Wind

The wind in the open
Tosses and hurls the leaves about the trees.

The wind in the mountains howls like hyenas
And wisps around the mountain tops.

The wind in the trees,
Whirls around the birds' ears and blows in.
It winds itself in and out of their legs.

When the sun and the wind meet
They make shadows like people dancing, moving swiftly.
The rain comes and kills them.

The flag droops on the flagpole.
Suddenly the wind draws up its breath
The flag flies around gaily and shows the Union Jack.

The saltant wind drives up the steep walls
And goes in through open windows.
The windows bang shut and crack into a hundred pieces.

Steven Gregory

18 'CAT' AND 'MOUS'

The title 'Cat and Mous' is really only an attempt to give a unity to something which has none. A sequence of 'Cat and Mous' poems will have nothing in common, but the title provides a jokey cohesion which can tempt the children.

The children are asked to suggest as many words as they can which contain either 'cat' or 'mous'. This is best done as a class lesson with the words written on the blackboard. Two lists will emerge containing words such as the following:

catapult	enormous
cataract	venomous
catseyes	moustache
catamaran	famous
category	mouse
catalogue	anonymous
catacombs	mousse

When the children run out of words you may be able to provide more, or they can look in dictionaries. This process alone is good for extending vocabulary and helping with spelling. There are many other groups of words that can be dealt with in the same way – for example, 'ages', 'able', 'ant'.

When the list is complete (or as complete as you wish), the children are then given the choice of any word about which to write a poem. This offers a wide range of subjects and every child should find at least one to attract him. To help them form a framework, it is useful to remind the children of techniques they have learnt – say, acrostics, riddles, rhyme schemes, patterns.

EXAMPLES

Catkins

A lazy remnant of early Spring,
When it was hot (but not too much),
And foliage on the trees made shadows on the ground
Which looked like a half-finished chess board.
With pure blue lying skies,
That pretended that last night's storm had not been
    there,
And still the willow weeps.

And people see nature
Through a rosy haze of laziness,
Where catkins take first place spinning in the breeze.
The home of dizzy beetles and greenfly.
And still the willow weeps.

Sarah Simpson

Famous

Moths fly to the lamp in ever decreasing circles,
Hypnotised, fascinated,
But when they fly too near they get scorched and
   burnt.
That is fame.

People flock like moths around fame's lamp,
Hating but loving its glare.
The one who survives being burnt attains fame.

You emerge made of tinsel, dressed in glitter,
With blinding rays and a gaudy mask sprayed with
   gold.
The filmy paper notes people pay you get burnt up in
   the lamp.
But the rain of old age puts out the lamp of fame
And the moths find another star to flock round.

Search in the tinsel to find your real self –
You'll only find ashes and dust.
That is fame.

Sarah Simpson

Moustache

Most men have them,
Others shave them off, or they grow them.
Useful to twiddle round when thoughtful,
Shaped to the style you want –
Tenderly sticking up,
Awfully showing off,
Covering a wart on a top lip,
Hoping everyone will admire you.
Every man should have one – a moustache.

Jansen Semmens

Anonymous

A name being nameless.
Surprising if you think
That man has nearly named everything
Except this.

Is it because it's weak and frail,
Or too strong and tough?
Perhaps it never had a chance
To show itself.

Jason Turner

(See also 'Caterpillar', page 75; and 'Catalogue', 'Enormous', and 'Catkin', pages 33 and 34.)

19 COMMUNAL POEMS

The communal poem, as its title suggests, is one to which a number of people have contributed a line or a verse. This is a good method of involving a group of children and can be achieved in a number of ways.

Begin by choosing a subject for the poem and putting it at the top of a piece of paper. The paper is then passed round from child to child, each one in turn adding a line. All the lines will be related to the subject and may follow logically on from those preceding, or may begin a new idea on the theme. The children find this fun and can all feel they have contributed a part of the final poem. The difference in styles can add to the texture and one child's idea can often lead others on to exciting developments.

If this is done with a whole class, three or four different poems can be going round at the same time, or the class can be divided into groups to write separate ones. It can of course be done during a writing session as an extra while other things are being written. The children merely pause from their work to add their lines when the paper is passed to them.

EXAMPLES

Light and Dark

Two separate forces that blend together,
The terror and joy of life.
The living of light and the death of dark.
Light jumps and dark crouches.
Light burns in the fire and dark lives in the ashes.
Light breaks and dark grows.
Light is a golden sound without sound,
Light moves silently and quickly, dark moves slowly and
    loudly.
A blanket of light, a blanket of dark,
Fight the other, one always wins in time.
A shadow is dark against the light,
Light is dark without the gusto.
The light brings hope and the dark brings sorrow,
Hand in hand they waltz the day away.
Light and dark blend to a shadow.

Written by children aged 10 years

Time

Slowly it passes by.
Some notice it, some do not.
Like a huge wheel rotating
It comes, leaves and is forgotten.
Everlasting,
Ever slowly,
There's never not a time.
Time kicks the hours away.
It goes fast when you're happy
And slowly when you're not,
Comes, goes, unnoticed.
Something never to be conquered,
Time the brother of infinity.
Dead or alive, time is still there.
It didn't start – it just is.
Through the sandglass time passes
Going backwards not forwards.
It goes slow but fast,
It flourishes past.
Time will never end
But lives its ticks away
And ticks away its life.

Written by children aged 10 years

Another variation on this is to have a large sheet of paper on the wall with a title at the top and a pen handy on a string. Any child at any time during the day/week can add a line to it. It is exciting to see it grow, the lines being added as, and when, the children feel like doing so. You could call this a kind of doodle or graffito poem.

A further very successful way of making a communal poem is to suggest a theme and give the first one or two lines as in the example below. Some discussion may be necessary beforehand for this kind of poem. A list of possible subjects for each verse can be written on the board. The children then choose from this list and cross off the items as they are chosen. This will ensure that there is a variety of different verses for the final poem.

The children write short poems (about six or eight lines long); they can write more than one poem on different items. The best are collected together and arranged in an appropriate order to make a long poem. This poem will have a unity given to it by the repetition of the first line or lines and will, of course, relate to the overall title.

EXAMPLE

Lumb Song

All of my attics used to sing:
Down the stairs, down the stairs
And down to the dark rooms
To see the rotting wools.
And the dusty smells of the old tattered mattresses.
Old statues and paintings show
Signs of pleasant work.

All of my windows used to sing:
Look through us, look through us,
Look, so our views are seen
And we do not get dusty.
Wash us so we are clean and fresh,
We do not care if you look in or out –
Only look, look.
If you do not look we will crack and mist.

All of my floorboards used to sing:
Walk upon me, walk upon me,
And I will creak with pleasure –
But just walk upon me, walk upon me.
Although I am old and dirty I still remain
And I will not collapse
Until my nails begin to bend,
So walk upon me, walk upon me.

All of my books used to sing:
Please read me,
Please read me –
Read me till my pages go ragged,
Read me till my story
Grows old.

All of my fireplaces used to shout:
Leave us alone, leave us alone.
We dislike being filled with rocks and dirt.
We do not like fire,
It burns our black friends, the chimneys.
We will burn the hand that puts the match to us.
Please leave us alone.

All of my cellars used to sing:
Come into me, come into me,
Collect my coal from my dim corners.
Come down my steep steps
And explore the dark rooms.
See the big spiders in their webs.
See the secret forgotten corners
Where the daring fairies play.

All of my windows used to sing:
Come look through us.
Come wipe the dusty old years away
And see through our glinting body.
Stare
At the open landscape.

All of my balconies used to sing:
Look out yonder to my valleys,
Look out yonder to my streams.
There you'll see the chickens feeding
And the trees rustling in the wind.
Water gliding
Slippery-slidey,
Stones and rocks,
Reeds and waterfalls.
My boney mountains,
My sweet valleys,
My crisp-cut cliffs
And my running streams.

All of my mountains used to say:
Study my rock:
Bring the geologist to research me,
My wildlife, my trees.
Bring the professor to protect me,
My jagged nooks.
Let the climber climb me and be proud to.
Bring life
For me to rejoice in.

Sharon Purves, Fiona Weir, Nicki Nathan,
Nikola Powell, Donal Crawford, Nicholas Brooks,
Petra Coveney, Christina Young

(See also 'Worlds', page 68.)

20 PATTERNS

Many poems that one reads are written to a pattern. It may be a simple repetition of a line which acts like a chorus to hold the poem together, or it may be more than that. A pattern, in the sense I mean, is like a framework which helps the poem almost to write itself. A poet who has often used this idea to very good effect is Pete Morgan, in such poems as 'Ring Song' and 'The Meatwork Saga' which can be found in his book *The Grey Mare Being the Better Steed* (Secker and Warburg). It can also be seen particularly in 'Who Killed the Leaves' by Ted Hughes in his book *Season Songs* (Faber and Faber). This last is derived from the old rhyme 'Who killed Cock Robin?'

The idea is to find a pattern out of which the poem can grow. Sometimes old nursery rhymes can provide this or a pattern can be made up. It is interesting to look through poetry books to find poems which belong to this kind. The following examples should give a clear indication of some of the possibilities.

EXAMPLES

Window

There once was a very small window,
hidden away in a corner of a room.

One day a small boy looked through the window
and saw a bright red fire engine.

An actress looked through the window
and saw her name in lights.

A farmer looked through the window
and saw a field of harvested wheat.

A housewife looked through the window
and saw a spotless kitchen.

A ghost looked through the window
and saw life.

A writer looked through the window
and saw a blank paper.

A press-man looked through the window
and saw his story on the front page.

A carpenter looked through the window
and saw a bed, varnished and ready to sell.

A gardener looked through the window
and saw a mowed lawn.

Then God looked through the window
and the window broke.

Steve Webber

Who Killed Who?

Who was the one who ate the apple?
I, said the worm.
Who was the one who ate the worm?
I, said the bird.
Who was the one who killed the bird?
I, said the boy, with my slingshot.
Who was the one who beat the boy?
I, said the headmaster.
Who killed the headmaster?
I, said the boy
With my 007 cap gun!

Anthony Freidin

I Say (ing), I Say (ing)

O Lordy, O Lordy,
I feel such woe,
I let the cat out
And it scratched me so.

O Lordy, O Lordy,
Why must it be me?
I spilt the beans
And now there's no tea.

O Lordy, O Lordy,
I'm so upset,
I dropped the milk bottle
And now my foot's wet.

O Lordy, O Lordy,
I am so sad,
I helped make the broth
And now it tastes bad.

O Lordy, O Lordy,
It pains me such,
I counted my chickens
And now there's too much.

O Lordy, O Lordy,
It isn't fair,
My arse is so good
The sun burnt me there.

O Lordy, O Lordy,
I think I'll retire,
I looked for the smoke
But got caught in the fire.

O Lordy, O Lordy,
I think I will die,
I tried to fool him –
He threw wool in my eye.

Donal Crawford

The Shadow of Death

I stood under the rainbow
And my shadow became the seven colours.
I stood by the boiling furnace
And my shadow turned red.
I stood in the greenhouse
And my shadow became green.
I stood under the noon sun
And it was short.
I stood under the dusk
And my shadow was long.
I stood under the moon
And my shadow became grey.
I died and there was no shadow,
Only death's.

Matthew Festenstein

21 SKIPPING RHYMES AND CHANTS

Playground games come and go during the school year; sometimes it is marbles, or conkers, sometimes jacks or hopscotch, but there are generally always some children skipping, even these days. Some of the old rhymes are still used in various versions and sometimes new ones will appear. As these are used by children at play they can also provide a good theme for creative writing.

One ingredient of skipping rhymes is the magical, almost riddle-like, quality which includes symbols and superstitions. Magic numbers – 3, 13, 7, 9 – abound, as do precious metals and stones – silver, gold, pearls, rubies and diamonds. Colours are often used and sometimes exotic places, as well as natural things like snow, trees, seasons. Birds which have a place in superstition, such as the robin, crow, raven, magpie and swan, also appear. All these occur in riddles and folk songs and are probably familiar to children.

Some discussion of the above ideas should act as a good preparation for writing, and a look at the Opies' book, *The Lore and Language of Schoolchildren*, will provide more examples. The children themselves can supply rhymes that they use and you may be able to look at these in some detail.

A poem by Alan Brownjohn called 'Skipping Rhyme' (which can be found in the anthology *As Large as Alone*, as well as other places) takes many of the ideas I have mentioned, but adds another dimension. The first verse uses a pattern of words which is completely reversed in the last verse.

First verse   Pain of the leaf, one two –
                  Word of the stone, three four –
                  Foot of the dark, pit of the hand
                  Heart of the cloud, five, six and
                  OUT!

Last verse   One, two, leaf of the pain
                  Three, four, stone of the word
                  Five, six, dark of the foot, hand of the pit
                  Cloud of the heart, and
                  OUT!

This is a good example of how to make words work for you and is more difficult to achieve than might appear. It is almost making each line into an anagram of itself, thus changing the meaning totally. The kind of words used is important and it can lead children towards a better understanding of how words are put together for an idea as well as giving them a fascination with manipulating them.

EXAMPLES

Skip Towards Death

Kill the seeds of life.
Eat them, eat them.
Destroy the brain of reason.
Confuse it, confuse it.
But let the hollow of death live.
Feed it.

Let the Devil mould it,
Then pass it on to man,
For man has got unlimited hate,
He will spread it if he can.

The seeds of life will kill,
They will eat you, eat you.
The reason of the brain
Will destroy you, confuse you.
But the hollow of life will bring death.
So starve it.

Donal Crawford

Zodiac Skipping Rhyme

Pisces caught two fish,
Aquarius caught none,
Gemini hit baby brother
And cooked the cakes for mum.

Seven gives me good luck,
Three gives me bad,
Five people in the rope,
First one's had.

Sagittarius hit a white goat,
Capricorn fell down dead,
Virgo went out hunting
And brought back Leo's head.

Three gives me good luck,
But seven gives me bad,
Five people in the rope,
First one's had.

Mary caught Cancer,
Cancer nipped the bull,
Taurus swallowed Scorpio
And Aries fooled them all.

Petra Coveney

Rhyme

When you throw a penny in the middle of a stone
Down comes a jelly bone.
No-one knows what I mean,
A penny in the stone
That's what I've seen.

Four is an unlucky number –
There are four ways out.
Don't even know which is the proper door.

Nine is a strange number –
When you throw the dice
You will lose the dime.

Thirteen is an incredible strange number –
You will be unlucky
When you walk through the forest.

Fifty is such a big number –
But I don't call it
Too much.

When you throw a penny in the middle of a stone
Down comes a jelly bone.
No-one knows what I mean,
A penny in the stone
That's what I've seen.

Lai Ling Leung

Skipping Rhyme

The corn grows,
Skip to it.
Its yellow lamps dazzle,
Pass it,
Don't tread it.
Let the crow peck the golden lamps.
Golden lamps, dirty, plain,
The scarecrow tired, forlorn,
The crows pull his straw out,
Then laugh.
The corn droops like a haggard woman,
Tread on it.
Out.

Jane Alden

Superstition

The waters were uneven,
The black and red ship 300 miles from land,
Death not far behind.
A sailor with a glass of sherry
Dipped in his finger to taste.
The one and only passenger
Rubbed his finger round the top of the glass.

Jane Alden

22 METAPHORS AND SIMILES

The difference between a simile and a metaphor is that a simile says a thing is *like* something else, and a metaphor says it *is* something else. Both demand that the user takes the creative step of putting together two very disparate ideas.

Similes are easier to deal with first as the children will probably be familiar with such sayings as – 'as like as two peas in a pod', 'as black as coal', or 'as cold as ice'. Discussion of some of these can serve two useful functions. Firstly, the children will become aware of the use of language to compare two things, and, secondly, it can be pointed out that many of these sayings are rather limited, not to say overused now. The way is then open for children to make their own comparisons on a more imaginative level. Some of them may have done this already in their writing and it is useful to quote from their own work. They should be told the word *simile* as they always enjoy knowing the correct term, and it can lend weight, in their eyes, to the work they are doing. It may be a good idea to have a specific subject or object about which they can think in some detail.

When the idea of using similes is first introduced you often find that the children overdo them, but this does not matter. They will learn to use this technique in moderation in later work.

EXAMPLES

Birds

Around me, beside me, inside my head,
Yellow beaked, black beaked, pin tipped eyes,
On that sea-bleached horizon in the sky,
Coming like deadly bees swarming from their hive.

Miles Greene

The Fingerprint

As it starts in the centre,
As it grows from in to out,
As a stone into the water
The shape becomes its size
Like a tree with its lines.

Stephen Buechner

Pond

Nothing stirred,
Only the reflections shivering in the wind
And the slime oozing its way to the edges.
A drooping branch hung
Like a dead man from a gibbet.
At the bottom
Long fallen leaves lay still
Like a forgotten cemetery.

Dominic Dowell

Fish

Fish,
Darting through the current,
Like arrows to a deathbed
Jabbing at the waves.

Jenny Tuffrey

Metaphors are a logical extension of the simile. It takes a rather bigger mental leap to say a thing *is* something else, but in the end I find metaphors more exciting. Children are quite capable of making this leap and a good way of helping them is to play the Furniture Game set out in Chapter 1. It might also help to take specific objects and see if the children can make them into metaphors for other things. A fine example of this is this poem by an eleven-year-old boy.

Summer

Summer is a cigarette,
Inhaled until it has nothing left to give,
And the charred remains are left
To make a smoky pillar of autumn.

Mark Nathan

This is an extended metaphor where the idea is continued in the same terms throughout the poem.

FURTHER EXAMPLES

Tramp

Sam is lying here
A silhouette of yellow dust.
This will be his home.

Louis Lyne

Candlelight

A flutter of light came from the flame of a candle.
I watched as the candle was lit,
The way it hurt.
And as I remembered each second of its dying light
A tear rolled down its melting body.
The light of the candle stuck in my head
Like drying wax.

Catriona Ferguson

The Cobra

His marks are honeycomb,
His eyes are like flying saucers,
His ribs stretch like elastic bands.
The curled teeth shining and ready for a victim.
His back patterns are stars in the moonlight.

Sharon Purves

Hyena

I howl around the mountains with my yellow chest
    glowing,
My black blobs a sign of beauty,
My eyes the oil ocean forever swirling.

Nikola Powell

23 COUNTING SYLLABLES

Before introducing children to the idea of writing poems to certain syllable counts it is advisable for them to have attempted Haiku, Tanka and Cinquains, probably in that order. They will then be more familiar with writing to a syllabic pattern and will be ready to experiment with their own systems.

In advising them of the possibility of setting themselves a form based on syllables you are really giving them the idea of a self-imposed discipline, encouraging them to experiment with their own forms. The ten syllable line is an obvious one to suggest to the children, but thereafter I feel they should be left to find their own line lengths, the rhythms and patterns that suit them individually.

With the ten syllable line I am not talking specifically of iambic pentameter which has a particular rhythm because this is quite difficult for children to grasp at first and should not be imposed. However, it is possible to ask for poems of ten syllable lines and many children will find this rewarding. They will even write some iambic pentameters as the rhythm is natural to many. At this point I should say that none of these forms ought to be considered as lessons in themselves; they are merely tools and frames for fashioning creative ideas. The ideas come first!

The following example is a communal poem written by ten-year-old children, each having started with the same first line (my own) as a way in and a link between verses. Each line has ten syllables.

Worlds

I have long walked in worlds unknown to you
Where landscapes start and finish in the same
Instant. Where seas flow over cracking ground,
Where whirlpools swallow and store knowledge which
Is attacked by parched thoughts and where logic
Can barely defend its own sanity.

I have long walked in worlds unknown to you
Where red floods cascade down tunnels of blue.
This is my globe, this is my paradise,
Yes mine, and it belongs to no-one else.

I have long walked in worlds unknown to you.
Birds fly through broken sunbeams in the mist,
Flowers are born with legs and arms to live.
A sky boat that moves with a breath of wind,
A person swims through the sea on a bird.

I have long walked in worlds unknown to you
Where the moon sweeps across the sky at night,
Where the sun rockets through the clouds at noon,
The world no-one has ever stepped upon
Apart from me. I rather disliked worlds.

I have long walked in worlds unknown to you
Where the rain does not fall to break the day,
Where the rays of sun burn up the days,
Where life will not die for sadness or good,
Because life is both – they live together.

I have long walked in worlds unknown to you
Where no creature has set foot before me,
Where moonlight is day and sunlight is night
And the stars are teeth in a gaping mouth.
Where the mountain river sings like a bird.
But I am old, these worlds have long been dead.

I have long walked in worlds unknown to you
Where the cock crows at the pitch of the black
And where the exit of peace now lies dead.
The day never comes and where men lived,
It is no longer a world but a mass.
The towers that stood fell into decay.
The money that was saved was the world's death.

I have long walked in worlds unknown to you
Where song has died and colour's fallen out
Away to a place where blue means nothing.
I have been in the happy worlds of peace,
But the worlds of peace died so very soon.
From that peace came war, the one of darkness,
The king of the black world beneath our mind –
He always conquers in these lands of mind.

I have long walked in worlds unknown to you
Where the sun is covered with sheets of black.
It took a hundred years until I came
Past the Atlantic through the seven seas.
I may be old but this world serves me right,
This earth is dark and grey and so remains.
There are no beams of light just disaster.
You shall not age because there is no pace.

Orson Nava, Callum Crawford, Richard Packer,
Julie Howson, Michael Hales, Rebecca Bazeley,
David Bailey, Matthew Festenstein, Darrol Kenworthy

(See also Chapter 25, page 76, on Sonnets.)

Here are a few examples of other poems which contain lines of nine, eight, or seven syllables. I have noticed that these three numbers seem to be particularly popular for line lengths and provide certain rhythmic patterns which children seem to use naturally. It may be noticed that some of the eight syllable lines fall naturally into the iambic meter. For example:

– I saw a hundred flaming guards
– I saw the sky alight with fire
– I saw a lioness give birth
– Where shadows are a man's best friend
– The stage returned its life once more

I wonder whether this links up with song rhythms, particularly folk songs, written in 4/4 time?

EXAMPLES

What Casca Saw

I saw a hundred ghastly women	(9)
Piled on one another.	(6)
I saw a hundred flaming guards	(8)
Marching towards the Capitol.	(8)
I saw the sky alight with fire	(8)
Spitting and crackling in its hearth.	(8)
I saw a lioness give birth	(8)
To twenty cubs or more.	(6)
I saw it raining blood this night,	(8)
Could it belong to Caesar?	(7)

Rebecca Bazeley

Anonymous

A warning to all the red waters	(9)
That have been bleached by the sun,	(7)
Black horizons on still waters.	(8)
I am a victim of this time	(8)
Where shadows are a man's best friend,	(8)
Where your home is your graveyard	(7)
As it is mine.	(4)
This is the way I now speak	(7)
On a stone slab above me.	(7)

Miles Greene

The Return

The dawn rose as the shadow returned,	(9)
The bare area came in sight.	(8)
The stage returned its life once more,	(8)
The masked area became unmasked	(9)
As the shadow had returned its share.	(9)

Catriona Ferguson

24 RHYMING

Some people still think that a poem is not a poem unless it rhymes, and because children are brought up on nursery rhymes they tend to use rhyme when first asked to write poems. They generally use it very badly. The many anthologies that used to be available in schools often contained poems that were little more than rhymes of the most facile kind. There are now many anthologies and volumes of poetry that treat children with more respect and try to extend their understanding, and where rhyme is shown to be more sophisticated than cats sitting on mats or chasing rats!

I make no apology for deliberately banning the use of rhyme when teaching a group of children for the first time – unless the rhymes occur naturally. Much later I reintroduce it when the children have become more aware of how to use words to their best advantage.

Explaining *Near Rhymes* is often a useful way of starting the children off again. Near rhymes are what the name suggests, where two words are similar enough in sound although they do not rhyme exactly. For example, a full rhyme would be *sand* with *hand*, but a near rhyme might be *sand* with *blend*, *bent* with *front*, or *summer* with *dimmer*. It can be the vowel sounds, or the consonants which make up the main part of the words, which are the same. There are some rules pertaining to hard or soft sounds, but at this level I do not feel it is necessary to stress them. Since one of the main problems with rhyming is that children spoil the flow and sense of their poems by using ridiculous words for the sake of rhymes, the introduction of near rhymes can give much greater freedom and wider choice.

EXAMPLES OF NEAR RHYMES

The Sun Murder

Mr Mistleshot's shot the *sun*.
He is to be *hung*
For every reason under the moon.
The weather will be as follows:
It'll pour for sure
And it certainly won't feign
To rain,
Whether you like it or not
It won't be hot
Because Mr Mistleshot's shot the sun.

Rebecca Bazeley

Clouds

Wet *colour*,
Has one *brother*,
Both make seeds grow to flowers,
And make the seed wait less hours
To *uncover*.

Allon Rimon

Extract from *The Four Men*

The man approached the place of the four *men*.
You come to take my sleep? said the *sleeper*,
I do not want your sleep, so sleep *again*.
You come to take my food? said the *eater*.

Darrol Kenworthy

The use of *Full Rhymes* can be gently encouraged after this and it may be that children will use both full and near rhymes, as can be seen in some of the examples above. Quite often a sparing use of rhyme in a poem which otherwise does not rhyme can be very effective. The rhymes act as emphasis and can also impart a musical and rhythmic sense to a poem. Children should be made aware that forcing a rhyme is bad, and indeed unnecessary, but using rhymes occasionally can add another dimension.

EXAMPLES

Schoolkeeper

The man who walked the tarmac ground
From here to the wire fence,
He knows his work will *die*
Just by the look in a child's *eye*.
Hands clenched under weather-beaten donkey jacket,
His eyes turn to the next door along
And fall to where
The broom and waxwork cup of *tea*
Are posted amongst the *greenery*.

Miles Greene

June

A light colour of crimson blossom *falls*,
The trees part with their leaves and begin *life*,
The birds crowned with their high tuned *calls*.
The windows reflected like a sour *knife*,
The ground rested with its surface melting.

Catriona Ferguson

Grandad

A quiet man,
A thinking man,
Always down in his *shed*
Working on a broken clock
Or fixing a car *instead*.
A quiet man,
A thinking man,
But now he's *dead*.

Rebecca Bazeley

A third use of rhyme is the *Internal Rhyme* which occurs where words are rhymed (full or near) but not at the ends of lines. These act as echoes within a poem and add to the texture and flow.

EXAMPLES
Caterpillar

Crawls like a miniature ocean,
Arriving at an unknown destination,
Tenderly feels around a *leaf*,
Every contact is *brief*, as if entering a naked flame.
Repeatedly moves its short legs,
Purposefully arches then straightens,
Ignorant of the prodding *hand*
Leans, and falls to *land* upon a leaf below.
Lazy, yet possessing a delightful beauty
Adrift in a world of dizziness –
Red stripes like bloodstained gashes on its back.

Mark Nathan

Tom Cat

In the middle of the night you hear a growl,
You know the tom cat is on the prowl.
Its fire eyes remind you of the devil.
Its *paws* are soft as velvet,
Its ice-like *claws*,
Its ears like horns.

Darius Saunders

When children are used to experimenting with rhyme it can be interesting for them to be encouraged to make up their own rhyme schemes using the traditional way of describing them, e.g. a, b, a, b, c, d, c, d . . . Once when a group of children wrote a riddle as a class they also determined what the rhyme scheme would be. They chose a, b, c, d, d, c, b, a; and enjoyed following their scheme, making use of near rhymes.

EXAMPLE
Communal Riddle

I once lay with the sand
But fire gave me life.
My body is cold, I have no heart.
I am hard yet hollow, you must treat me gently,
I am empty but full; once full now empty.
I shatter and destroy, but intend no hurt,
I blur and distort the human eye,
You can break the heart I never had.

(A bottle)

25 SONNETS

If anyone had suggested to me a few years ago that I might have eleven-year-old children writing sonnets I should have laughed at the idea. However, after teaching the same group of children for two years I found they had progressed so far, and their enthusiasm was so great, that I decided to try them on sonnets as an experiment.

I felt the lesson required a more lengthy build-up than usual so I wrote out two of the more accessible Shakespearean sonnets on the board – 'When I do count the clock that tells the time', and 'My mistress' eyes are nothing like the sun'. We looked at them one at a time.

I read the sonnet and explained any difficulties of meaning, but principally asked the children to explain what it was about. When this was done I asked them what they noticed about the form. Since by now they knew quite a lot about poetry, they were quickly able to spot the rhyme scheme and the ten syllable lines. I then explained the rhythm of each line by marking the feet in the usual way – ∪/∪/∪/∪/∪/ – and by tapping the rhythm while speaking the lines. We enjoyed a short period of time trying to speak to each other solely in iambic pentameters, which made something of a game out of fixing the rhythm in their minds. They had to be steeped in the rhythm in order to be able to escape its constraints and concentrate on what they wanted to say when it came to writing.

I then told them of some different sonnet rhyme schemes. They were able to choose which type of sonnet they would write and I gave them a free choice of subject. This particular group were never short of ideas for their writing so I did not always prepare a subject. With many groups it may be necessary to talk around a particular idea.

Here are three examples of completed sonnets by these top primary children. All of them used the Shakespearean form. I would say that it was a valid exercise although some of the spontaneity is missing at times; but it was a difficult task! All the children enjoyed doing it although, by the very nature of the work involved, not all managed to complete their sonnets.

They may never write another sonnet in their lives but I feel this lesson was worth doing. It opened up a further influence on their work and it certainly made them think hard about words, especially rhymes which, at their reasonably advanced state of development in poetry, they were not content to use to the detriment of their poems. A large amount of re-working was constantly going on to try to make the lines right rhythmically; the rhymes worked, and above all the poems said what they wanted to say.

EXAMPLES

The Four Men

The man approached the place of the four men.
You come to take my sleep? said the sleeper,
I do not want your sleep, so sleep again.
You come to take my food? said the eater,
I do not want your food, I have enough.
Do you come for my thoughts? said the thinker,
I do not want your thoughts, your thoughts may bluff.
Do you come for my drink? said the drinker,
I have no thirst so drink all that you can.
I am the joker and I come to fool,
I shall keep joking as when life began.
I'll take your heart and stuff it till it's full,
I'll take your brains and carve them with my knife,
And what I come for, I shall steal – your life.

Darrol Kenworthy

Sonnet

Hundreds of people shouting to the world,
Too many speeches to let people breathe,
Too many hopes in vicious flags unfurled.
Eventually for blood they all will seethe
And war and bombs will start to smother us.
And on Death's pillow which will be uplifted
You'll see without regalia or fuss,
How we the nations civilised have drifted
To dust and hell upon this arid plain.
But from this desert new races will grow
And godliness and peace will live again,
Live men not dead machines will reap and sow.
Then they shall learn to love one another
And so to curse the man who hates his brother.

Matthew Festenstein

Sonnet I

The tramp has walked these many weary miles
And now lies down to rest in a hayloft
On bales of hay that lie stacked into piles
Put by the road. The hay feels very soft.
Through London and the country he has been,
Sleeping in the alleys and the street
And in old houses he by chance had seen,
But every kind of weather he would greet.
His ragged coat shows many signs of wear,
His once white trousers show up mud and grit,
Around his head hang strands of lank, black hair,
A cigarette is in his mouth unlit.
As night came down the next day looked like rain,
But in the morning he moves on again.

Timothy Cousins

26 FINDING A THEME

It is the finding of ideas that is usually the hardest part of teaching poetry. Many of the other chapters in this book have suggested specific themes and here I propose to put forward a few more general thoughts on the subject.

Direct observation is a tried and trusted way of encouraging children to write: bringing in objects; bottles containing cotton wool soaked in different solutions to hand round for writing about smell; looking at pictures, slides or films; listening to music or tape recordings; taking children out to a park, a high street, market, or anywhere they can write while experiencing their surroundings. Any way that involves direct use of the five senses can lead to good poems and the more used to writing children are, the more interesting will be the results.

EXAMPLES

Storm

Cold water balls fall in heavy currents
Upon the varnished land,
And the circling scraping slide of feet
Moves wetly over the puddled ground.
The relentless wind circles the shiny wet pebbles
Causing an unheard whistling as it passes through.
It makes sea-like waves
As it gusts into the water-drenched air.
The massive grey clouds
Shedding great bolts of energy.
The clouds give thundering claps
As they watch arrows of light
Turn dead objects into living infernos.

Orson Nava

Ship in a Bottle

Floating on an aimless current,
A constant reminder that we'll never reach port.
Hope in a bottle is not easy to find
And happiness was lost in a storm.

Matthew Festenstein

Forest Ocean

Enclosed in an ocean of rippling green
But no fishes swim here.
Insects crawl unseen, unheard
Like water nymphs flitting
A sea within a pond.
A duck quacks and flies away
Frightened by your presence,
Ripples form on sea and pond,
Flying fish make very birdlike noises.

Michael Corti

Bull

Maddened by a man and his tempter.
Dancing around like the tell-tale birds
Which used to circle him.
An arena of hatred
Reminding him of his now forbidden freedom.
A five foot terror and yet passive inside.
If given the chance he would go off and wallow in mud.

Christina Young

Projects can always give rise to some creative writing and because the children have been studying a subject in detail the poems they write will contain information which will improve their writing, if used well. Having a factual knowledge of a subject will ensure a more specific approach which is to be encouraged. There is almost nothing worse than the woolly generalisations that are often presented.

EXAMPLES

Tournament

The herald sounded his bugle twice, then thrice.
As the last note faded away
A ripple of anticipation ran through the crowd.
The knights got on their armoured horses.
The knights' squires
Passed up their big heavy shields and lances.
The gallop of the horses, and the upturned turf
Where the great black stallions have beaten and
    plundered.

Jason Turner

Yggdrasil Is Dying

Yggdrasil is dying,
It is going, going.
From the curse of mighty Thor's hammer?
It is going, going.
From the mischief of the evil Loki?
It is going, going.
From Surtur's cold fire?
It is going, going.
No!
It is dying from the Nid Hog
Gnawing through its single root.
It is eating its wooden heart.
There is no blood left.

Donal Crawford

How the Round Table was Completed

A chilled circle slab of coldness.
The core had been finished
But the outline was still to begin.
The chisel had yet to strike
The meaning of the table.
Sir Gawain
Unknown to the group assembled
Went forth to perform his deed.
And when he returned
In the air they felt victory,
The hammer,
The chisel,
A new blow.
Gradually the outline was done,
The round table was completed.

Rita Monjardino

Different facets of the same word can be investigated, an idea which involves taking a subject, for example LIGHT, and allowing the children to write on any aspect of the theme. The word or words chosen must offer many possibilities, although it may be argued that all nouns fall into this category.

If we take the example LIGHT, the idea would be to make a list on the blackboard of all the different kinds of light. These suggestions should mainly come from the children.

For example, they might propose candle, electric, gas, lighthouses, torches, matches, open fires, forest fires, sunlight, moonlight, starlight, reflected light, signals, traffic lights, headlamps, glowworms, luminous paint, the spectrum, Blackpool lights, street lamps and so on.

The children then have a wide choice of titles for their poems and each one will be essentially different from the others, although they all fall under the same heading. It can be useful to ask the children to suggest a theme, as they will feel it is more their own idea. Other such themes might include the four elements – earth, air, fire and water, or trees, darkness, wood, metal, heat, cold. (*Note:* The essential thing to remember, however, is that there are no special themes for poetry. Poetry can be about absolutely anything, from the most mundane material object or experience to the highest philosophical thought!)

EXAMPLES

Searchlight

Searchlight shining through the blackness
Picking out the plane's location,
Shooting it down with the whole spectrum.
Always swivelling its white shadow
Against the sound of falling bombs.

Matthew Festenstein

The Moonlit Circle

It reflects on the water, the moon,
A circle of shining ripples.
A tin can is thrown in from the pier,
It lands in the moonlit circle.
Water fills in through the opening,
The can floats out from the circle.

Julie Howson

The Reflected Light

The light shone in her face,
Red, green, purple and white.
It shone straight into her eyes.
She pulled a face and tightly shut her eyes.

It hurt but she didn't say.
Turn it off please, she said.
A man put a board in the way,
The light reflected on to it.
The light dazzled, flickered and went off.
The reflection went too.

Wendy Ellis

(See also 'Candlelight', page 67.)

Reading poems in various volumes and anthologies will often spark off an idea. Seeing what angles poets have taken on different subjects can sometimes suggest something you had not previously thought of. This is a quite legitimate way of obtaining ideas as long as they are not presented to the children in a restricted form which results in poor imitations of the original poem.

Using lines from famous poems as the first lines of poems can produce interesting results. If the line is good it will set a tone for the rest of the poem. In some cases a whole verse may be used. (This exercise is not something to attempt very often, nor, for that matter, should any of the ideas or ways be used to excess. Variety of approach is always best.)

Perhaps three or four different lines can be given to the children, thus affording them a choice. A further interest can be excited by reading the original poems *after* the children have written their own – not before, however, as they should be free from all associations.

EXAMPLES
(line from *The Thought-Fox* by Ted Hughes)

'I imagine this midnight moment's forest'
Where you can hear the owl
Calling through the silent trees.
The gaudy gnarlness of the rows of firewood
Growing and dying in the night aromas.

The stillness of forgotten time.
The emptiness filled with life,
Shunted and roused as the daylight approaches.
My midnight moment's forest
Destroyed by its creator.

The same place is another
As the sun surrounds it.
My own image thrived in this lushness of forests,
And died in its own world of immortality.

Rebecca Luff

(line from *Wind* by Ted Hughes)

'This house has been far out at sea all night.'
The waves were tall, the house was small.
We sank once or twice, but resurfaced.
But the lifeguard stood shaking his fist
Because the house was blocking the light.

David Bailey

(verse from *Neutral Tones* by Thomas Hardy)

'We stood by a pond that winter day,
And the sun was white, as though chidden of god.
And a few leaves lay on the starving sod;
– They had fallen from an ash, and were gray.'

Gray from the time they had left their home,
Their dwelling far off the ground.
We left them there untouched, unfound,
On the sod by the pond, so dark and alone.

And there set apart from the world they will lie,
Dropped from the tree of ecstasy.
None of us thinks this is fantasy,
For in the well of our hearts lives a lonely cry.

Donal Crawford

27 TEACHING POINTS

❀ 1   The teacher should be interested in, and enthusiastic about, poetry otherwise the children themselves will be indifferent towards it. This involves the teacher in reading poetry for pleasure, listening to poetry on radio and television and, if possible, going to poetry readings. Trying to write yourself (whether you show anyone or not) will help to increase your own enjoyment, and your awareness of technical points and difficulties. For anyone who would like to know more about the different forms used in poetry there are a few books which set them out briefly but clearly. One of the best, I have found, is *The Poet's Manual and Rhyming Dictionary* by Frances Stillman (Thames and Hudson). The rhyming dictionary is an unnecessary extra on the whole, but the manual is well worth having.

❀ 2   Ban the use of such endings as '. . . and then I woke up', and 'The End'. It is clear if a piece of writing is finished, and all dream sequences are usually better left in dream. I think children often write these endings to provide a sort of security. They may experience the need to return to reality before they leave the piece but I feel it should be stopped as it mars so many good ideas. They should be encouraged to feel at ease in their fantasy worlds.

❀ 3   Have plenty of dictionaries of all types and grades of difficulty available in the room, and encourage children to use them.

❀ 4   Have as many anthologies and individual volumes of poetry as you can available on a shelf in the classroom where children may freely borrow them. Encourage children to read poems as well as novels from the school library.

❀ 5   Read plenty of poems to the children, sometimes just for fun, sometimes to be discussed, sometimes as a starting off point for some writing. If used in the last way it is often better to read a number of poems on a theme, otherwise many children will only re-hash what you have read.

❀ 6   It is very good to have volunteers to read to the class poems which they have found in books from the library or at home. I have known nine-year-old children who began by reading Spike Milligan, Ogden Nash and Lewis Carroll (all perfectly all right), but graduated in their taste and sophistication by the age of eleven to choosing poems by Hardy, Yeats and MacNeice. There never seems to be a shortage of volunteers. Not only does this encourage the children to read poetry – they must read a number of poems in order to choose one – but it helps their ability to read out loud, something which is often overlooked these days.

❀ 7   It is useful to keep a class poetry book where the best work from each session is mounted. The work is typed out and this acts as an encouragement to all; there is nothing like seeing one's work in print! During the year you should make sure that every child is represented in the book, but you must also set a high standard.

Each session the work from the previous lesson should be read out by you or by the children and it is useful if you can all comment on why **the** poems are good. Children learn from these comments.

The book should be attractive and left around the classroom so that the children can read it at any time. It is probably better to put as many pieces in as you can at the beginning as this will be more encouraging. Standards can be raised as you go on. One-finger typists take heart – you will soon improve and it is worth the effort!

❀ 8   I would advise against using creative writing cards as a general rule. They exist supposedly to help teachers, but are most often used as an easy way out. There may be occasion to use them sometimes as a change, but they are very limiting unless a child has a well-developed ability to write and then, of course, they should not be necessary. It is really so much better if you, as the teacher, can provide the ideas. A card is unlikely to stimulate and enthuse a child in the same way that a teacher can, and used to excess, as with any method, will soon become tedious.

❀ 9   When the children are writing it is sometimes a good idea if you try to write something yourself. Tell them you are going to try, and be prepared to let them hear your attempt. We are constantly expecting children to write to order and it is a very sobering experience to face up to the same difficulties that they encounter.

❀ 10 Do not expect each child to produce a good piece of work every time. No poet can possibly write a masterpiece with every poem. There will be failures. Sometimes writers are just not in the mood, for some reason the ideas will not come or will not fall into place. Tell the children this, and they will not use it as an excuse; it is more likely to encourage.

❀ 11 It takes time to write a good poem. Very occasionally it comes quickly, but you are lucky if it does, so do not expect much if you only allow twenty minutes for writing. If possible, arrange your day so that children who want to can go on working on their poems.

❀ 12 Encourage children to re-work poems as a 'real' poet does. Nibble away at the poem until it comes right.

❀ 13 Until the children are used to writing poems it will be necessary for you to go through much of their work and help them put it into lines, commenting on your reasons. You may find that there are accidental full, near, or internal rhymes, or that a natural rhythm pattern makes the line breaks obvious. Taking out odd words or rearranging sentences can make all the difference, and turn what is essentially prose into poetry. After doing this a few times with a child, you can ask him to do it for himself.

EXAMPLE

The boy was as free as a bird that had been trapped in a cage and as lively as a leaf, which is all wrinkled and dry. He sits in the corner of a room where the door is locked and so is his mind but in a different way. His mind is locked on the life he had once led and the freedom he had once had. He sits there not moving and will soon become an everlasting part of the room. Now he is dead and all that remains is a watch that doesn't tell the time but it tells a story which is the story I've just told you.

(by a boy aged 10)

On the next page is one way of making this piece into a poem.

The Boy

Free as a bird trapped in a cage,
Lively as a leaf wrinkled and dry,
He sits in the corner of a room.
The door is locked and so is his mind,
Locked on the life he once had led,
Locked on the freedom he once had known,
He becomes an everlasting part of the room.
Dead now, and all that remains
Is a watch that doesn't tell the time.
It tells a story –
This story.

Most of the lines have a rhythm created by a pattern of four strong beats ending on a strong syllable, but this pattern is occasionally varied, on lines three, seven and the last two, at points where there are definite pauses indicated by meaning and punctuation. These variations help to improve the poem. A little repetition in lines five and six, and the last two, helps to bind it together. The last two lines are shorter and break naturally to emphasise the last line for a more dramatic finish than in the original. Nothing has been drastically altered, but a child can learn a tremendous amount from this exercise.

❀ 14 Never prescribe a set length of writing you expect the children to do in a session. Too many teachers say, 'I want a page by lunchtime', or similar stipulations. A piece of writing is finished when it is finished and that might be at three lines or thirty-three. This obviously demands some initiative from the children but they soon understand. To aim at the highest possible standard is what is important and a few well thought-out, successful lines are better than pages of mediocre work or worse.

❀ 15 Let the children have rough books to work in. They should not have to be bothered about spelling and neatness when they are writing. If you are encouraging them to re-work their poems there will inevitably be things to cross out and words to add in. A writer's notebook is often messy. The time to write out a fair copy in the English book is when the poem is in its final version. Then spellings should be correct and handwriting neat. If the children have to think about that when first writing, it will interfere with their spontaneity.

❧ 16　Never type out children's work with wrong spellings, it is far too patronising. Always correct them. Besides, other children will be reading the poems and it is bad policy to present anything which is incorrect.

❧ 17　It is also not advisable to use bad examples from children's work to illustrate what should not be done. Teaching by positive examples is better and will help to build up confidence.

❧ 18　If it is at all possible, working in silence produces better poems. There is no doubt about this. Everyone needs room to think and this means the least possible distraction. Long queues of children with completed work should therefore be avoided. I have always explained that I prefer to read their poems at home where I can sit down and enjoy them. This is usually appreciated. It is useful to make sure that there is other work organised for those children to do when they have finished or they can be encouraged to write another poem. This will also leave the teacher free to give help on specific points where needed.

❧ 19　Contact with living writers can be a great stimulus to the children and there are several ways of achieving this in school.

(a)　The Writers in Schools scheme, until recently run by the Arts Council, was set up in 1969 to assist schools to have writers in to read to, or work with, children. The fee and the date for a visit are agreed with the writer and application is then made, at least two weeks in advance, for a subsidy towards the cost. This scheme is now (since 1 April 1980) operated by the Regional Arts Associations and a list of addresses and the areas served can be found on pages 91–3. Normally half the fee will be reimbursed to the school after the event and travelling expenses can also be reclaimed where long distances are involved. (Overnight accommodation, however, will not be covered.) For further information and any regional variations, write to the local Arts Association.

A word of warning here: do not work your writer *too* hard on the visit. One long session in a morning or afternoon is really enough. Nobody but a teacher is capable of going non-stop through a day and even then it can be quite a strain.

(b)　The Arvon Foundation is an arts venture with two centres, one in Devon and one in Yorkshire. Courses are set up for five days or a weekend, and the children spend the time under the guidance of two tutors who are practising writers. There is a guest reader during the course as well.

If you are thinking of taking children to Arvon, it is as well for you to attend one of the open courses arranged for adults over the summer months to find out how it operates. Your LEA may pay your course fees; it is worth asking. You may also be able to obtain money from your LEA to subsidise the children. For further information about Arvon write to:

The Centre Director	or	The Centre Director
The Arvon Foundation		The Arvon Foundation
Totleigh Barton Manor		Lumb Bank
Sheepwash		Heptonstall
Nr Okehampton		Nr Hebden Bridge
Devon		West Yorkshire

(c) W. H. Smith sponsor a scheme called Poets in Schools and will pay for two poets to spend three days in a school to work with children. For more information write to:

> The Education Secretary
> The Poetry Society
> 21 Earl's Court Square
> London SW5

❀ 20   You may soon reach the point of wanting to enter the children's work in some of the national competitions. By far the best of these, which covers the whole age range from five to sixteen, is the W. H. Smith Children's Literary Competition (previously the *Daily Mirror* Children's Literary Competition). The standard is high and each year a book is published containing the winning entries. Poems, prose and plays are all eligible. A distinguished panel of judges makes the final choices and there are certificates of merit for individual children, as well as prizes for winners and schools. For further information write to:

> Children's Literary Competition
> W. H. Smith and Co. Ltd
> 10 New Fetter Lane
> London EC4

WRITERS IN SCHOOLS SCHEME

Regional Arts Associations (England)

Eastern Arts Association
Literature Officer
8/9 Bridge Street
Cambridge
CB2 1UA
(Tel.: 0223 357596/7/8)

Bedfordshire, Cambridgeshire, Essex, Hertfordshire, Norfolk and Suffolk

East Midlands Arts Association
Literature Officer
Mountfields House
Forest Road
Loughborough
Leicestershire
LE11 3HU
(Tel.: 0509 218292)

Derbyshire (excluding High Peak District), Leicestershire, Northamptonshire, Nottinghamshire, Buckinghamshire

Greater London Arts Association
Literature Officer
25/31 Tavistock Place
London
WC1H 9SF
(Tel.: 01 388 2211)

The area of the 32 London Boroughs and the City of London

Lincolnshire and Humberside Arts
Literature Officer
St Hugh's
Newport
Lincoln
LN1 3DN
(Tel.: 0522 33555)

Lincolnshire and Humberside

Merseyside Arts Association
Literature Officer
Bluecoat Chambers
School Lane
Liverpool
L1 3BX
(Tel.: 051 709 0671)

Metropolitan County of
Merseyside, District of West
Lancashire, Ellesmere Port and
Halton Districts of Cheshire

Northern Arts
Literature Officer
10 Osborne Terrace
Newcastle upon Tyne
NE2 1NZ
(Tel.: 0632 816334)

Cleveland, Cumbria, Durham,
Northumberland, Metropolitan
County of Tyne and Wear

North West Arts
Literature Officer
12 Harter Street
Manchester
M1 6HY
(Tel.: 061 228 3062)

Greater Manchester, High Peak
District of Derbyshire,
Lancashire (except District of
West Lancashire), Cheshire
(except Ellesmere Port and
Halton Districts)

Southern Arts Association
Literature Officer
19 Southgate Street
Winchester
SO23 7EB
(Tel.: 0962 55099)

Berkshire, Hampshire, Isle of
Wight, Oxfordshire, West
Sussex, Wiltshire, Districts of
Bournemouth, Christchurch
and Poole

South East Arts Association
Literature Officer
9/10 Crescent Road
Tunbridge Wells
Kent
TN1 2LU
(Tel.: 0892 41666)

Kent, Surrey and East Sussex

South West Arts
Literature Officer
Bradninch Place
Gandy Street
Exeter
Devon
EX4 3LS
(Tel.: 0392 218188)

Avon, Cornwall, Devon, Dorset
(except Districts of
Bournemouth, Christchurch
and Poole), Gloucestershire,
Somerset

West Midlands Arts
Literature Officer
Brunswick Terrace
Stafford
ST16 1BZ
(Tel.: 0785 59231)

County of Hereford and
Worcester, Metropolitan
County of West Midlands,
Shropshire, Staffordshire,
Warwickshire

Yorkshire Arts Association
Literature Officer
Glyde House
Glydegate
Bradford
Yorkshire
BD5 0BQ
(Tel.: 0274 723051)

North Yorkshire, South
Yorkshire, West Yorkshire

For details of schemes existing in Wales, Scotland and Ireland,
write to the appropriate Arts Councils:
Welsh Arts Council
Holst House
9 Museum Place
Cardiff
CF1 3NX
(Tel.: 0222 394711)

Scottish Arts Council
19 Charlotte Street
Edinburgh
EH2 4DF
(Tel.: 031 226 6051)

Arts Council of Northern Ireland
181A Stranmillis Road
Belfast
BT2 5DU
(Tel.: 0232 663591)

Arts Council of Eire
70 Merrion Square
Dublin 2
Republic of Ireland
(Tel.: 0001 764685)

SELECTED BOOKLIST

Anthologies   Editors

Junior Voices, the first book, the second book,
   the third book, the fourth book   Geoffrey Summerfield
(Penguin)

Voices, the first book, the second book,
   the third book   Geoffrey Summerfield
(Penguin)

The English Project, Stage One (6 books)   Various
(Ward Lock)

The English Project, Stage Two (6 books)   Various
(Ward Lock)

Wordscapes   Barry Maybury
(Oxford University Press)

Thoughtshapes   Barry Maybury
(Oxford University Press)

Bandwagon   Barry Maybury
(Oxford University Press)

Bandstand   Barry Maybury
(Oxford University Press)

Touchstones 1, 2, 3, 4, and 5   M. G. and P. Benton
(Hodder and Stoughton)

Happenings 1 and 2   Maurice Wollman
(Harrap)   and Alice Austin

Poems of the Sixties   F. E. S. Finn
(John Murray)

The Puffin Book of Magic Verse   Charles Causley
(Kestrel, hardback; Puffin, paper)

The Puffin Book of Salt-Sea Verse   Charles Causley
(Kestrel, hardback; Puffin, paper)

I Like This Poem   Kaye Webb
(Penguin/Puffin)

Here and Human   F. E. S. Finn
(John Murray)

Poets of Our Time   F. E. S. Finn
(John Murray)

Worlds   Geoffrey Summerfield
(Penguin)

Rhyme and Rhythm	Red Book	James Gibson
	Blue Book	and Raymond Wilson
	Green Book	
	Yellow Book	
(Macmillan)		

Famous Poems of the Twentieth Century   W. G. Bebbington
(Schofield and Sims)

INSIDE OUTSIDE

Sky with Diamonds   Frank Plimmer
(Macmillan)

Fair on a Beautiful Morning   Frank Plimmer
(Macmillan)

If I had a Hammer   Frank Plimmer
(Macmillan)

As Large as Alone   Christopher Copeman
(Macmillan)   and James Gibson

Selected Shorter Poems of Thomas Hardy   John Wain
(Macmillan)

Soundings   Kit Wright
(Heinemann)

First I Say This   Alan Brownjohn
(Hutchinson Educational)

Modern Poets One   Jim Hunter
(Faber and Faber)

Volumes of Poetry   **Author**

Season Songs   Ted Hughes
(Faber and Faber)

The Hawk in the Rain   Ted Hughes
(Faber and Faber)

Poetry in the Making – a teaching anthology   Ted Hughes
(Faber and Faber)

Brownjohn's Beasts   Alan Brownjohn
(Macmillan)

Rabbiting On   Kit Wright
(Armada Lion)

CHATTO POETS FOR THE YOUNG (Series)   Various
(Chatto and Windus)

Add to these almost any other volume of poetry, however adult in content; poetry
speaks to all ages.

Selected list of dictionaries

	Publisher
The Word Hunter's Companion: A First Thesaurus	Basil Blackwell
A Simplified Dictionary	Schofield and Sims
The Nelson Contemporary English Dictionary	Thomas Nelson
The Oxford School Dictionary	Oxford University Press
Longman Junior English Dictionary	Longman
Black's Writing Dictionary	A and C Black
Illustrated Junior Dictionary	Heinemann Educational
The Concise Oxford Dictionary	Oxford University Press